Thirty-Six Ways
to Love

by Charles Prince

*All booklets are published thanks to the
generous support of the members of the
Catholic Truth Society*

CATHOLIC TRUTH SOCIETY
PUBLISHERS TO THE HOLY SEE

Contents

———•———

Introduction

————◆————

*T*his booklet is the result of a bet I once made with a young man. In a discussion we were having, we realised that the everyday words for expressing love and friendship are generally badly used. We ended up by agreeing we'd need to make a collection of these words. "Let's see which of us can find the most!" we said.

Personally, I find that the expression "I love you" is one of the emptiest phrases in the English language. Other languages may express shades of difference, but ours makes no distinction between loving chocolate and loving a person.

I've seldom said "I love you" to anyone. There are several reasons for this. Perhaps I didn't want to commit myself, knowing that my love has always been ephemeral and I didn't want to get entangled and, in the end, hurt someone. Then I realised that even though I didn't actually say the "magic words",

I could still express my friendship, my consideration, goodwill, attachment - plenty of things I lived out every day, and that through all of that, without even realising it, I was loving people.

Some time after that I was on my way to see that same young man. On the train, I remembered our bet, and that I hadn't yet done anything about it. So just a few minutes from the station, I borrowed a pen from the person sitting next to me, rescued a luggage-label from the depths of a pocket, and began to write my list. I got to the bottom of the label and wrote down the margins, and when there was no room for any more words I counted them: thirty-six! I felt as if I'd discovered thirty-six ways out. It was my revelation of the day: it's love that enables us to find a way through, and there's no shortage of ways of putting it into practice!

So here's the list, though certainly not an exhaustive one, and I've expanded a little on each verb.

I would really like it if every reader corrected it, added in his or her own way of putting love into practice, changed the order, or added still more verbs. It's all part of our inheritance as human beings, not someone's private property - especially not mine - and we are called to live like that; nobody can excuse themselves if they want to be happy.

This essay might be dedicated to all human beings, starting with all those who have chosen to love and to live. It might also be dedicated to all those who have kept their hearts childlike, as well as to all the mothers and wives who have fought to keep their hearts womanlike, and to all the men who have tried to discover and respect the mystery of woman.

Many young people have helped me in this work, among them couples preparing for marriage. This booklet can be used as a 36-day retreat. That would give time to "digest" each of the words, and see where we ourselves are along this path of humanisation.

It's not so much a method as an examination of conscience to help us not to get discouraged along the way.

1. Respect

―――――•≫•≪•―――――

R especting a person is the first and most basic way of loving. Without respect, you can't enter into love.

There stands before you someone who exists independently of you. You can't reduce him and you must consent to make room for him.

Out of politeness, you let him go first, quite simply; that means that you welcome his existence.

You can't enter into his life without his consent, just as you can't reject him from your own life without rejecting his right to be considered someone lovable.

He has the right to live and to know the truth, but he can only demand what is actually necessary to him.

It's also important that you make him respect you; the love he has for you will enable him to discover what's fair. He will learn to distinguish between what he has a right to, and what is given to him freely.

His life includes so many aspects; his past, his desires, his weaknesses, his qualities... You're free to take them on board or not, but don't forget that he is all of those things, and sometimes you only have to reject one of them to make him feel rejected altogether.

Behind and beyond his outward appearances, he has an absolute worth, and the greatness of his existence as a human being is something indestructible. He is a subject that you can never reduce to an object or a thing without wounding him.

You can't, for example, reduce him to his body alone, or to his soul alone, because he is both. He is not a material thing that you can change into something else, but a living person, bearing within him a thirst for the infinite that rebels against all limitations.

You will have to respect his choices, because they are what make him develop, and he can only go forward by facing the consequences of his actions. So allow him the right, and the opportunity, to make mistakes.

2. Open

O pen your door, put a door-stop there to keep it open, and make sure it never shuts again, so that people can come in and leave when they want.

Make room for the other person, make yourself available so that he can find you behind your barricades, in your solitude.

Say what you have to say, but don't close the discussion: make the other person feel sufficiently at his ease to put in a word too.

Choose to open your heart and keep it open whatever happens, knowing that you can make use of everything to love: what awes you, what wounds you, what leaves you cold as well as what burns you up. You can make use of everything to open your heart wider: "Love makes a fire of every kind of wood." You have to choose to do it. That's the wager of love - to make a terrific fire out of anything at all, even things that seem not to be flamable.

The hardest thing to fight against is the temptation to shut the door. It's so simple, so easy to do, but it's the beginning of death. You can't consent to that, even though in certain situations you realise you are obliged to keep your distance.

So stay open, remain capable of loving, waiting for the opportunity to take another step, or waiting for a response from your friend in reward for your patience. Like that, your open heart will be a source of hope for your friend and for all those who seek to love. They need that stability so as not to get discouraged, so that they can overcome every kind of despair and hardness.

3. Wait

Open the future by consenting to be poor and in want, and also consenting to be dependent and limited.

Recognise your need, your weakness and your want, and admit that alone you can't do very much; then humbly ask the person who can provide the answer.

Keep your desire open, without despairing, without saying straight off: "That would be too good, that could never happen to me."

You have to keep your desire, not wanting to satisfy it at all costs by helping yourself, but waiting quietly for the right moment, when it will take shape. Your desire will be purified until it becomes a true desire: that of receiving your friend himself, before receiving what he gives you.

Wait, without doing anything else, patiently, convinced that the more truly you have waited, the better the final meeting will be.

Give your friend time to reply, without forcing him or upsetting him. He may not yet be ready to give himself, because he's never before found anyone ready to receive him.

4. Welcome

You've opened the door and let your friend come in. You make room for him, to show him that he matters and that he's at home in your house.

You wanted that love, that attention. Now you have it, and you're responsible for it.

Welcoming means making that person your own, it's a movement of your heart to embrace and receive a new reality or a new truth to live with.

Because it's new it needs a new place. Don't worry: your capacity for receiving is infinite - all you have to do is want to.

What you desired is there before you: what are you going to do with it? You were waiting for one thing, and now here is something else, unknown, unexpected; a delay or an unforeseen arrival, and here it is. You can easily walk away, but you can also receive it and welcome it.

Perhaps it wasn't what you wanted, or perhaps it's a lot more than you were expecting; but it is yours if you want it.

You can go and look elsewhere for something better, or else you can welcome this, here and now.

5. Look

———✦———

See, and then look the other person in the face. Let your naked heart appear in your face, lay it open to the other person's eyes, so as to tell him: "Yes, you are important to me, you are a treasure, a marvel."

Look, and at the same time take the risk of being seen, of being recognised.

Open your eyes in a positive gaze at the other person. A waiting look, that refuses to admit failure, and even before reaching that point, refuses to believe that the other won't or can't give more.

Look, being proud to be able to say: "It's my face, these are my eyes, I have no others. I'm not hiding anything and I'm not afraid to meet you, to take the risk that you may hurt me."

Look further than you see, beyond outward appearances, good qualities and faults. Join the other person where he is most himself, gaze on the mystery he represents, knowing that you will never get to the end of it because what is essential is invisible to the outward eye.

Then it is a look that makes the other grow, impels him to love himself, to have confidence in himself and look with his own eyes, as if he were seeing for the first time; then the world becomes beautiful, colours appear and the light becomes dazzling.

The scales of prejudice and fear fall from his eyes, to be replaced by a gaze that marvels and questions.

It is no longer a gaze that seeks itself, but one that has found what is good, found the right place to be.

6. Listen

Listen in silence, going beyond particular words and circumstances to what the other person carries in the depths of his heart: his questions, his expectations, which perhaps he himself is not aware, but which are very much part of him.

Welcome his words, however clumsy they may be, as the expression of what he is, of what he is looking for.

Listen to his question, which is always the same: "Do you love me?"

Be really there, so that the other person doesn't feel alone or that he's just engaging in a monologue, even if you are incapable of answering.

Receive his words in their raw state, just as they are, respecting his reasons for breaking out of his silence.

But first you need to listen to what you yourself carry in the depths of your own heart: overcoming your fears, and even profiting from your own sadnesses, all of which are signs pointing to the absence of your heart's desire. *Cœur qui soupire n'a pas ce qu'il désire* - the heart that sighs does not have what it desires.

Hear your own desires and sort them into order, so that you can then be more single-minded in your search and in your capacity for welcoming others.

Then you will hear your friend's life awakening, bursting forth, wanting to soar in flight without limits.

7. Understand

———◆◆◆———

What you have heard or perceived, you now need to assimilate, take in, make your own - even if it seems crazy, way outside your normal classifications and parameters.

Perhaps it's something that won't fit into any known file. Open a new one for it and let yourself be imprinted, marked, by this unknown person who may hurt you or question your established ways.

Behind the clumsiness of his words, understand what is really affecting or wounding the other person, and then tell him in your own words what you have understood, so he can confirm that you've understood him properly. Then be ready to listen again, as best you can, to what he has inside him, without immediately slamming down a judgement or a solution that he won't be able to take because it doesn't fit his situation.

You need to widen your space for understanding by pushing back the boundaries of your fears, your freedom, and what you find pleasing.

Difference will enrich you, because everyone who takes the trouble to speak brings a part of the truth. Even if his reasoning is false, he brings a real desire to understand and sort out his life.

8. Ask

———◆———

*I*t's hard to depend on someone, but it's even harder to admit that you haven't understood, or that you're in need of something, and then make up your mind to beg, to recognise that you are not self-sufficient and that you need other people's help.

It means humbly submitting to being helped - without standing back and letting the other person do it all for you - so as to be able to give to others in your turn. It means consenting to put yourself in someone's debt, because the fact that you've had the courage to show someone your neediness is going to create a real link between you and them.

Ask, in order to give the other person the opportunity to give. Make the other person feel needed, without making him feel he's being used. Let him decide for himself what to give and how he's going to give it.

Ask again, to renew your desire, and to tell the other person once more that you do genuinely want to receive something from him, that it's not some whim of yours but something that really will enable you to grow towards autonomy.

Ask your friend always to tell you, before the sun goes down, anything about you that has hurt him. Like that, silence won't turn poisonous but will be a sign that all is well.

9. Trust

———◆———

*T*rusting someone, confiding to him some project you have very much at heart, or entrusting him with yourself, always means taking a risk.

It also means recognising the other as another self, raising him to your own level, especially when you know his weaknesses. By trusting him, you make him your equal, a partner with you, a prolongation of your hand, your eyes, and above all your heart.

Trust is friendship's most valuable treasure. It is the fruit of friendship, and at the same time the very heart of every friendship.

It may exist quite simply because circumstances permit it and leave no room for doubt. But trust is a gift, a deliberate choice that you will have to make when doubt arises. There will almost always be an area of uncertainty, and if you want to continue to love, you will have to take that risk with all its consequences.

And even if it ends in failure, you can always be proud that you trusted someone. Because the very act of trusting him is itself a victory; it's always a heroic act. So the actual result doesn't matter so much.

Your victory will also be a victory for the person you trusted. You enabled him to surpass himself and prove to himself not only that he was capable of not betraying your trust in him, but also his own capacity to live out something new, to give himself to a point where he never knew he could.

Trust, like love, is unconditional; it's a gift of the self. Trusting someone else makes you grow, and makes the other person grow too, regardless of the outcome.

———⊷⊶———

10. Carry

More and more, you need broad shoulders, not only to be able to carry yourself, but to be able to carry other people too, in their difficulties and weaknesses.

"Carrying" also means suffering in silence when some problem is impossible to solve, not trying to run away from it or pretend the problem doesn't exist, but keeping your heart open, even though you are wounded to the heart.

Taking all that on board means raising up on high the burden that you have been dragging along, so as not to risk stumbling over it again. Because as long as that burden remains unacknowledged, rejected, you won't be able to achieve a unified personality. You have to love not *in spite* of that, but *with* that.

When you take up the burden of your own mistakes, you're recognising yourself for what you are: they are *your* mistakes. And you owe it to yourself to sort them out, instead of forcing others to carry them for you. Your friend can carry them, but it's not for him to take them from you. And you shouldn't let him help you if you are able to sort your mistakes out yourself. The opposite is also true: you shouldn't try to take over your friend's responsibilities.

Carrying a secret that someone has confided to you means carrying that person as a mother carries her child. And if you reveal that secret to someone else, you are wounding the person who trusted you, because the secret was not yours, it was entrusted to your care.

Carry the silence of the person you love, welcoming it as a sign of his love, his respect for you, instead of feeling forgotten or rejected. That means allowing him to love you in the way that he has freely decided to do.

11. Bear

Continue bearing, even though it may hurt, so as to absorb whatever your friend has unloaded onto you. He has had sufficient trust in you to believe that you could not only carry all of your own burdens but also that you could relieve him of some of his.

Sometimes he has unloaded his own hurt onto you violently, without asking first, certain that you would accept it. He simply wanted to destroy his own despair, his near-certainty that no-one had enough unselfish love to be able to enter into his solitude.

If he hurt you, don't ask why, because you might wound him even more. You need to know that there isn't always a reason for evil, but there is always a search for good behind every action someone performs. You need to bear with what looks like senselessness in order to keep what matters: communion with the other person.

If you can't carry any more, say so. It's no use overestimating your capacity. You have the right not to be superhuman, because if you collapse, you would risk hurting your friend even more and it would then be still harder for you to carry him.

It is a blessed thing to choose to stay with your friend no matter what happens, happy simply to be there for him, so that he understands that his life is important to you, perhaps even more important than yours.

12. Forgive

———◆———

*T*ell him that the fact he has hurt you does not stop you from loving him and choosing him all over again, because you too are capable of hurting people like that or even worse.

If you forgive him you'll enable him to be reconciled to his own heart, by erasing his hurt. Continue to give yourself to him through the hurt he has caused you and because of it. Forgiving him means answering him when he appeals to you, even if without realising it we do it clumsily, to love him more.

You will be bringing a new dimension to your friendship, by recalling the basic fact about it: you love your friend and there is nothing that can stop you from loving him. Everything else is secondary to that.

Forgiving means picking up the broken pieces of a vase your guest has smashed before he has time to bend down for them, as if you'd broken it yourself. And doing it so as not to leave him alone with his responsibility, to set him free from blame and self-loathing.

Never demand that he says sorry, because your love for him can't be conditional. He will need time to realise how much he has hurt you.

But, depending on how deep your friendship goes, you can tell him about your wound. Then give him time to leave his self-blame behind and rejoin you whenever he can. He is still too intent on himself to be able to look beyond his own failure and love someone else.

When all's said and done, there may well be nothing to forgive. Look and see whether the injustice that seems to have been inflicted on you is objective, or if in fact it comes from rights you've invented for yourself. If so, you now have the opportunity to learn to be poor, and to beg him to forgive you.

And if your friend finds it hard to forgive you, tell him you're sorry again. Like that you will show him that you don't want to live without him and that he is important to you.

13. Offer

Offering means first of all showing, with deeds, all the disinterested love of your heart. But it also means giving yourself, abandoning yourself like a child into the hands of the person you love.

Offering means making your life not just a distribution-point but, quite simply, a gift. Because until you have given yourself you have not really given anything. Only the gift of yourself can satisfy your friend.

No more barricades, no more mistrust. Total transparency, revealing measureless trust and confidence.

You no longer belong to yourself, because you've given yourself to him. You are leading your life as belonging to him. You will never take back that gift.

No longer belonging to yourself, having given yourself totally to another, is the cause of your greatest happiness. Perhaps it's the greatest freedom that can possibly be experienced: being free from yourself, making use of yourself to enrich other people.

Make your life into bread for him, good bread to nourish him and give him back his strength. Your life can be wholesome food, sustaining, easily digestible, welcome.

He will want more of that good bread, until he himself learns to become nourishment in the same way, solid food to offer to those who hunger.

---

14. Recognise

———✦———

In your life you go forward with the aid of landmarks or reference-points, reliable signs to tell you who you are travelling with and how you should act.

Sometimes you get lost, no longer knowing who you are, searching for yourself. Where did you go wrong?

You can recognise all those you meet, even if you've never seen them before, because they've each got two eyes, two ears... they're human beings like yourself, part of the human nature you possess. They're like you, and that's your first reason for feeling a bond of solidarity with them.

You can recognise yourself in the person you've chosen. He has become like you, while the person you didn't choose remains strange to you. So you now need to be reborn, renewed, by welcoming what's new in him.

You need to recognise yourself just as you are, face to face with the person you love, to enable him to be himself likewise. It's difficult to show yourself with all your defects, to recognise your faults, but that sets your friend free from his own self-blame.

In a relationship, because there are no perfect beings, there is always the risk of wounding the other. Recognising each other's faults enables each of you to look at difficulties calmly, taking them at their true value.

15. Embrace

When you love someone, embracing means touching their whole life, telling them that your love embraces everything - their past, their present and their future.

Only then will your kiss be a truthful one, conveying everything you have inside: your choice and your commitment to consider the person you love as a treasure to be cherished.

The fact of placing your lips upon them shows the importance you give them. It is a free gesture, given without expecting anything in exchange, just to express your love, your attention, your presence, as if to say "I'm here for you, and for you alone."

A kiss, a contact between two faces, the most personal part of the body, means a meeting at a deep level between two hearts, each exalting and magnifying the other.

The unnoticed kiss on the forehead of your sleeping child; the kiss you give your mother to show her how much you honour her and thank her for all she has given you; the kiss you give your spouse to show your love and respect; the kiss you give your friend to tell him he has a place in your life; these are so many ways of expressing your love, manifesting it in a physical, graphic way, beyond any kind of false embarrassment.

———⟨•⟩———

16. Bless

———⪼⪻———

*T*o bless is to desire the good of the person you choose, without claiming anything for yourself. It's an unselfish desire, a concern for the other person to be great without ever changing or lessening his goodness, enabling him to give the best of himself freely.

Blessing him means helping him to become fruitful in every dimension of his life and soul. It means making him better by first making him experience his goodness, everything in him that is positive, his desire to live, find his place in the world, grow, improve, and also his desire to give freely, to be a source for someone else, to be useful, and his desire to love to the extreme of giving his life. All of this is something that he can't invent for himself. It can only come from a friend who loves him, freely, for what he is.

It means wishing him the best he can hope for and thanking him for existing, because without him you wouldn't be here today.

You have already experienced his fruitfulness for yourself, and you know that that fruitfulness can only increase, for himself, for you and for others.

Blessing someone is magnifying and exalting them while making yourself small before them.

———✦———

17. Serve

———◆◆◆———

Put your whole self into a simple act of service, which may sometimes require an effort, to be able to say that the other person is more important than you, consenting to make his concern, his project your own. Then you welcome that project as if it were yours, and put your nose to the grindstone, wholeheartedly, to make it work.

The other person has trusted you, and you need to be faithful. The treasure he has entrusted to you in his heart, that has decided risking disappointment, that you could be like another self to him.

Perhaps the service you do seems servile; that doesn't matter, because if you want to love someone, what he asks of you is not what's important - it's up to him to choose, and he can even choose the way in which he wants that service done if necessary.

What matters is that he can count on you unreservedly, knowing that you won't ask for anything at all in return. Your service is given freely, becoming a source of joy. And that joy is all the greater because nobody can take it from you. You are proud to be able to give, renouncing beforehand every kind of recompense, even a thank-you.

18. Set Free

---

*E*nable the other person to be himself, bringing him face to face again with his own freedom.

His life belongs to him, and he has the right to decide for himself what he wants to make of it, because he alone is responsible for it. But too many things still tie him down to the earth and keep him in a sort of constraint that he's sometimes not even aware of. Fears, feelings of guilt, resentments, doubts and even false ideas are there, shutting him up inside himself. Only the truth coming from a friend's mouth can set him free to be himself.

You can experience no greater joy than being yourself and enabling your friend to be himself, consenting to love himself and love others with what he is.

That implies that you have also undertaken the labour of life and love in yourself, so that your friend can be at ease in your presence.

It's not easy to get rid of all the deceptions which are not precisely intended, but which are in fact present in our affections. You make your fear of not being loved into an excuse for hiding the thing you think the other person will dislike about you. And yet your friend was only waiting for you to show him the truth, to become sincere and transparent himself.

19. Awaken

*A*waken in the other person a thirst to live more, to tackle life with zest, helping him to discover the joy of standing upright.

Push him a little further so that he's no longer content to remain half-asleep without realising it.

Explode your friend's dreams or imaginings, if he still finds it hard to put his feet on the ground, or still prefers to cover his face because it is the easiest or most comfortable thing to do.

It demands a lot of vigilance, a strong determination to go for what is essential; maintaining a state of constant questioning, to keep going along the way without stopping.

It also means keeping up your concern to rest while going forward. That's the secret of all who fight and win: they are straining towards victory, and rest in that certainty.

It is true that you can't rest unless the danger is distant, but the goal itself gives you rest. The only danger is to fall asleep without realising it. That's the end of the fight: your limbs grow stiff and you die in the cold of the night, or else the enemy takes you unawares and you have no time to react.

Which is why you can never be content to let your friend live below his full capacity. But you can't hold it against him if he doesn't yet know what his capacities are, or underestimates himself. His hope of life can only come from revitalising encounters with someone who wants the best for him.

You will enable him to live truly when you yourself have made up your mind to stay on your feet, when you have refused to desert or go to sleep like him.

20. Lift Up

———

Lift your friend back on his feet when he's fallen down. No matter that you've often lifted him up before, taking him by the hand and telling him "You're great": he didn't take it in. He still needs your hand because he hasn't yet made up his own mind to stand upright, hold his head high and say, "This is me, here I am with all my weaknesses and mistakes."

Your love bears within itself the hope that he will one day stand up and stay standing, in spite of all his wounds and weaknesses. In spite of, but also *with* all of that, he can stand upright.

By recognising and admitting his own weakness he will experience strength and find a cure. He will be freed from his fear of not being loved. He will recognise the way he is, and accept that that is the way forward for him. Falling down isn't the worst thing that can happen: the worst thing is failing to get up again.

The first time, it's your friend who lifts you up, because you hadn't even thought you would ever stand again. You saw your fall as an act of fate and you'd resigned yourself to it. You thought, "What's the point of getting up, if I'm only going to fall down again?" And your friend got you on your feet so that you would know it was possible after all, and be able to do the same for others.

Think of all those people who let themselves die. Their thirst for life faded into despair, and never again became a deliberately chosen desire. Their thirst for life sank to rest because they were waiting for someone to choose for them and take over their lives.

You have to tell your friend that his choice is his alone, and that his life will only begin when he decides to live it himself, to stand on his own feet and walk.

Some people are physically crippled but continue to walk in their minds, keeping their will to live going with the limited means that remain to them.

21. Encourage

Give your friend courage, because life is stronger than anything else. Awaken in him a rage, a fiery zest for living life to the full.

You can give him that courage even when you yourself are becalmed. Your love will enable you to mobilise all your forces, but only if you love your friend more than yourself.

The desire to live is the most violent of battles. Refusal to live is an act of cowardice that you must never let your friend commit.

Bring him back to his choice of life, his freedom. His decision is his alone, and you can't choose for him.

He can't live by proxy, through another person, or like a parasite, sucking out life from others. He wants to be a source of strength. He knows that, but still finds it hard to believe.

Nothing is ever lost, there's everything to go for, as long as a spark of life remains. There have been cases of people in a coma who, hearing someone saying something stupid beside their bed, have woken up out of sheer anger and packed their family out of the room. They needed that sort of encouragement to hang on to life.

All other kinds of discouragement stem from an initial failure to choose to live. The choice of life, the choice to live, is what enables you to take possession of your own vitality, to be patient, and to choose again in order to sharpen your desire to live out your life.

That is where you realise that living, in the most real sense, means loving. Because when that point is touched by death, even what's left alive stops making sense.

22. Value

———◆———

Your friend's deepest desire is to know what he is worth to you, and what place he holds in your heart, in your life.

No-one has ever told him what he's truly worth. Up till now it's always been by competing and fighting that he's tried to win himself a place, the first place, a prince's place.

Only your positive outlook on him and his actions, including his failures, can enable him to make a scale of values for himself.

It is a person's heart, in the first place, that thirsts to be valued, and not his capacity for work or learning.

Only the gift of himself has value. It's the intention of the heart, even before the gift is made into deeds, that you have to look at first. Once the intention is there, you must never cast doubt on it or question it again. And if the intention is obviously bad, that will be your opportunity to purify and redirect it.

So it's the love he shows that gives him most value in other people's eyes and in his own. That's where he experiences himself as a source. That first victory, deciding to give before he looked to receive anything, will bring many others in its wake.

Value him through his action, but also through his words, which he finds hard to get out, because he's afraid of looking ridiculous. Listen to him even if he's incomprehensible, even if you could put it much better than he can; let him discover for himself what he's worth.

23. Guess

Guessing implies that you know your friend really well and are in the habit of putting yourself in his place, living in him, in communion with him.

When you have truly listened to him you find you can finish sentences he starts, and even tell him what he has deep down inside, that he hadn't yet put into words. But let him express himself; he's big enough to speak for himself.

You sense his inner state in spite of the barricades he puts up, and you meet him there with so much love that he lets himself be found. That implies a lot of trust between you, and it also implies that you see him positively.

You guess his desires and take initiatives that he may perhaps think are rather bold, but he can't object to them because he's happy that you have guessed him, and especially that you know him so well. He discovers in you another self.

Before each encounter, ask yourself how to express the greatness of the other person or how to make him become greater. You won't let yourself be distracted by the sort of superficial chit-chat that hides so many important things. You'll go straight to the point, so that he never goes away disappointed.

———⊶⊷———

24. Reveal

Look at the person you love with eyes that build him up, eyes full of calm expectation and hope, eyes that show him what he really is.

Be attentive to what he is, beyond the way he looks on the outside, and beyond his current capacities, which can only grow.

You need to reveal to him his good qualities first of all, even if the general tendency is towards pride. Because what most often gets the upper hand is inhibition, arising from underestimating oneself. Between elation and depression about oneself, there is a happy medium, which only a friend can reveal.

You can ask your friend (without making him ask you to do the same) to tell you about your faults at an opportune moment, and still better, to remind you to remain poor.

That can be a mutual pact you make in order to become greater together. Otherwise you risk imitating the ostrich, perpetually hiding from problems. Then you may try to be kind and avoid arguments, up until the day that you cross the line of what you can put up with, and suddenly say things that seriously hurt.

That pact of transparency is crucial in building up true friendship. Frankly admitting the poverty of your character is nothing in comparison with silence, which gives rise to imagining the worst and allows misunderstandings to increase.

25. Anticipate

Anticipating enables you to face up to life instead of dragging along behind it, always a bit late.

Get there first, before you're asked for something. If you think someone's going to ask you for a mountain, be prepared to offer them the whole planet, even though it doesn't belong to you (and, to be honest, nor does the mountain).

You're scared that someone's going to eat into your time or your possessions or whatever is most personal to you. Go and offer them the very best part of it.

You could get up in the morning with a desire to re-invent the day, asking yourself what you could do to love. Mobilise all your energy to spread a bit of happiness around you, and play a joke to break up the solemn nature of everyday life, or to make sure you don't risk taking yourself too seriously.

Anticipate difficulties, because "forewarned is fore-armed". Accepting defeat in advance will make you calmer when it comes. "Too bad, better luck next time!" You'll survive!

Like in a game when you refuse to be a bad loser, you're proud of holding on till the bitter end. In your own way you've won, with your strength, your legs and your speed. There's no real competition, because each individual is different. Even for two identical twins, the chances are not the same. What matters is that each person goes forward - walking, on his knees, crawling, but still going forward.

Anticipating failure means finding another way of getting around the problem, choosing the best method of attaining the goal.

You can also anticipate victory by acting like a winner from the start. It's funny how our attitude is always focused on the risk of losing, when films get us used to stories which almost always turn out well.

The word "almost" is a terrible one, enough to make you give up. Think about "always" and you find you've gone over to the winning side.

And so you can anticipate your friend, who doesn't dare to tell you what he has in his heart, or what his greatest need is. Be generous, because everything that's not given is wasted. Never miss the opportunity of showing him your love, because sometimes it may be the last chance you'll have.

26. Accompany

Accompanying your friend doesn't mean doing things for him or instead of him, but with him, so that you don't risk diminishing his commitment. Enable him to become autonomous little by little, as his self-confidence grows.

You can always do things yourself, but it's better to get him to do them, to give his self-confidence a chance to take root.

At each step, every time he surpasses himself, he'll discover a new aspect of himself. He'll learn more and more what he's capable of, and the points where he has to recognise his limitations.

That will enable him to walk forward confidently along the tightrope of life.

Your helping hand will make him understand that it's possible, but that he will have to try it alone to be sure of himself.

See if you can manage to give him the impression that he has done it all himself, like a grown-up. That step forward, that new achievement, came from him, even if he did get a bit of help. But it was he who took the decision to do it, and he can do it again.

———◆———

27. Lead

———⊷⊶———

L eading means accompanying your friend by going ahead of him.

You can tell him the route to follow and let him get on with it, or you can open up the path and warn him of the dangerous bits.

But above all, you can show him the end of the road, because that is what will give him the desire to get going and walk with you.

By going ahead of him, you're bearing witness to an immense discovery waiting at the end of a journey, that you have already made. That's why your friend trusts you.

At that point he is in a very vulnerable state, when you could hurt him badly.

But if you keep your fear of wounding him alive, you will come to know what's best for him. And if necessary you'll get out of the way rather than lead him to where he's bound to fail.

Never forget that you're not leading him to yourself, but further. You are the intermediary. You mustn't lead him astray by making him believe that you constitute his happiness.

It's true that you contribute to it, but you can't keep him for yourself or stifle him. What you can do is provide him with air to breathe and a place to rest, so as to send him on towards a greater freedom when he will choose you as someone he doesn't want to be without, rather than someone he cannot be without.

28. Educate

Your friend is free, and so any learning he does will only be as a result of his personal choice. It's true that you can oblige him to go forward, but what you should do is help him to make choices that will release him from his state of indecision, so that his "yes" is a true "yes" and his "no" is a true "no".

Educating him is still leading him, but with co-operation on his part that goes deeper, because it requires openness of heart.

The goal of this education is perfect freedom, which is autonomous with regard to choice and also regarding the means to be employed.

That freedom is to be sought through a progressive rectification of the mind and will. Your friend needs to achieve a mind that looks and listens, and a heart that is not put off by difficulties.

What most needs rectifying is the will, because it is the will that chooses the path to be taken, as well as the means proposed to it by the mind.

All his personal vitality, which tends to be dispersed and scattered, needs to be channelled and guided in the right direction so that it can blossom fully.

He has never suspected how strong his life can be if it is unified around the most vital thing of all: the gift of self and the search for truth.

The help your friend asks you for after expressing his difficulties, however clearly or confusedly, leads you to help him almost as a father would.

Being a father means, above all, being able to look to what is good for the other person before thinking of what's good for yourself. It's an attitude of freely consenting to be a source of life without looking for anything in return, not even the satisfaction of seeing results.

29. Reassure

<hr/>

Your friend needs a firm shoulder to lean on so that he can take a step forward while remaining himself. He is petrified by fear or anguish about some danger that could arise.

You need to learn to be there for him right where he is, at the moment he's living in, foreseeing the difficulties and finding the right way through.

He may foresee the worst and find the most effective way to ensure success. He may also foresee and accept defeat, knowing that he has nothing to lose and everything to win.

You need to step back and orientate yourself, to be able to tackle problems. It's exhausting to be constantly tense expecting new problems.

Sufficient unto the day is the evil thereof. Tomorrow can take care of itself - and you can say the same of every minute. Every night when you go to bed you need to let go, come clean, because the concern you are holding onto no longer belongs to you - or doesn't belong to you yet.

In this way after you've overcome your own fears, you can reassure your friend who is beginning to lose his foothold. Sometimes you won't feel particularly secure yourself, but helping him will help you as well.

---

30. Bring Peace

*B*ring peace to your friend: help him to be where he is, his feet firmly on the ground. The ground has not yet given way, the sun has risen today as it does every day, the birds are singing, and you are there. His wound is there too, but peace wins because life is always stronger.

You will pass on your stronger life to your friend when he is weak. You can make him taste your victory as a pledge of his own.

It's a way of saying "I love you" in answer to your friend's most urgent question: "Have you a place for me, where I can stop and rest?"

Bringing him peace means consoling him, soothing his burns, applying ointment to his wounds to help them heal over, and telling him, "Calm down, take a breath." He may be beside himself as a result of trials, anxiety, despair or feelings of guilt, so that he can no longer feel the joy of simply being wholly himself, being there.

Sometimes there is no immediate solution, and he needs to learn patience.

Patience is a real treasure, because it leads on to hope, to a rejection of fatalism and resignation. It also leads to confidence and peace of mind, and will enable him to discover a new outlook on life.

———◆———

31. Feel Compassion

Suffer with your friend as if his suffering were your own.

You do it anyway, without being able to help it, for someone in your family or someone who's very close to you. But you can also suffer with someone you feel no instinctive affection for, if you recognise his suffering as your own.

You can embrace that suffering as a part of the person you love, to break down a wall that normally separates you. Because it is a part of him which may be the reason why you reject him or why he withdraws from you.

All you have to do is tell yourself that you may be in the same situation one day, and that you'd want to have someone near you then. But compassion can never be out of self-interest; either it is given freely, or it doesn't exist.

Carrying his unhappiness means allowing him to be completely himself with you; it's very hard to be totally sincere and beg for the other person's help or presence. You always think that nobody will be interested or want to take you in, and you close yourself up and hide your face, keeping your suffering to yourself. But if suffering can't be shared in a friendship, where can it be shared?

The grace given to married couples, for example, enables them to suffer with each other's sufferings. Even before turning to a psychologist or counsellor of some sort, the couple themselves can and should face up to their shared weaknesses and wounds.

If they do, their unity will be still closer and deeper, because they will each experience the strength and fruitfulness of their limitless love.

That's your opportunity to show your friend your faithfulness and to prove to him that you have really chosen him, in good times as in bad, and that you will stay by him no matter what happens.

That is really being father or mother to him, a new way of loving that takes love still further.

32. Choose

Choice is not always between two things; it may be in one direction only: you choose or don't choose, you commit yourself or don't commit yourself.

There are so many things in your life that you haven't chosen and that you're still just dragging along... but it's not too late! Even when something is imposed on you, you're still free to choose it.

The simple fact of your birth, that somebody else chose for you, is something that you can choose, and take possession of your life. If you do, you're being reborn, and choosing to live today, this moment.

What you are, the place where you live, the work that you do well or not so well... you can choose all of that.

And, beyond everything else, you can choose the people you love. Perhaps they have changed; you welcomed them into your life without any difficulty, but now you can actually choose them, and you need to.

The friend whom you choose begins to become part of your life. He's not just an item to be taken into account, but a real being, whom you don't want to live without from now on.

Your life includes and takes on his life, so that he becomes part of you, a prolongation of yourself. And everything that he lives through, you live through with him.

Like that, you're choosing to spread out your life, not like an octopus dragging everything to itself, but like a poor person who is thirsty to live as much as possible and drinks in Life in all its manifestations. And the best manifestation is in your friend.

Your choice depends on your capacity for welcoming, and that depends on the love you have within you. What it all boils down to is that life is not a lottery where you hope for the winning number: there isn't one.

And you don't just choose the first person to come along, because choosing takes time.

However, you know when you've found a spring of water that can quench your thirst, unlike all the others that could only disappoint you. It brings you new strength, enabling you to make further choices.

———◆———

33. Espouse

———— ◦•◦ ————

Like water that takes on, espouses, the shape of the bottle it's poured into, you espouse the person you have decided to let into your life, and whose life you have decided to get into. You take on his life, recognise him as a part of yourself.

Like choosing, espousing in this way is a voluntary act which you undertake, all the more forcefully because you are totally free.

It takes time to be free enough to choose the other person regardless of the good he does you and the hurt he may still cause you. Regardless of your own weaknesses and confusions.

You espouse him little by little, down to the smallest details, taking them in as they come to light, and you recognise them as your own. You take on his good qualities and his faults, his openness and his limitations, until you are completely one with him.

That is the goal: to be one with him. To live a profound communion so that neither of you is alone any more. To make an alliance, which you hope is irrevocable, in which you refuse from now on to live without each other. "I" and "you" become "we".

The alliance is always fragile, because it is based, not on ties of flesh and blood but on your desire to choose each other again every day of your lives.

You are both still alone in your being, but each of your lives is filled with the presence of the other, who becomes and remains a secret. And that secret finally brings you out of your respective solitudes.

34. Remain

Remaining means living, staying there, settling yourself in your friend's heart to make it your dwelling-place. Drinking at the well-spring of his heart, everything he lives by. Sharing his life in communion with him, sharing everything he is, so as never to leave it aside again. All of that is the answer to your own deepest thirst, which is to live ever more.

It's true that it isn't possible to share absolutely everything materially, but if you live in that heart-to-heart way nothing can be unknown to either one of you, because everything is shared, is common property. And so you each live twice over, while each continuing to live your own lives and staying yourselves.

As long as you don't achieve that communion of life, there will always be a risk of jealousy or frustration, and a temptation to live a double life.

You can do lots of things, while still dwelling within each other's heart: there you each hold the other.

It's a mutual contract that demands a large amount of vigilance and determination. You need to have already embarked on it to be able to see everything else in relation to it, and you need to take care to stay there, and to return as soon as you realise you have been distracted from it.

For example, if your friend starts telling you about the day he's had, whether unbelievable, superb, or even disastrous, help him to get back down to earth and take off his helmet, since his only responsibility is to take command of his heart again and retrieve all the little bits that have become dispersed.

Or, again, never forget that it isn't what you do that should motivate you, but what you are. In other words, it's not the place you're going to that matters, but the place where you dwell, the place you always come back to. You can only leave it on one condition: if you are at the same time always there.

35. Accept

————◆————

Welcome, reach out, take on, make part of you...

Up until now you refused to make love into the whole reason for your existence. It seemed too simple, too good to be true. And now, having finally accepted it, has your heart remained open, no matter what?

You accepted responsibility for those whom you made your own, so that their imperfections didn't stop you from welcoming them and choosing them.

So many walls have crumbled since the day you accepted your need to respect those around you and respect yourself.

You accepted your limitations, your rhythm, your wounds, what you are by nature, and other people, just as they are.

You accepted the fact that you weren't the best, but quite simply aiming to be better.

Accept, now, the need to be ever ready to begin again from zero; accept that you can't take anything as achieved once and for all, and that you need to continue to fight endlessly so that love will continue to be love. It can't be boxed up or kept in one place. It would be altogether too comfortable if you could fit it into a frame, if you could just keep it for when you wanted to make use of it.

You can't foresee what it will become, but you can choose to make it grow constantly greater.

Love is your friend, and at the same time it is waiting for you as the fruit of your friendship.

Accept the fact that you are poor, because you can't take possession of love; like truth, it will always be greater than you.

Accept that you are neither truth nor love, but someone who drinks of them constantly. And accept that you are loved, that there's nothing left for you to do but that, while you remain powerless, bereft, trusting in your friend's love for you.

———◦●◦———

36. Last Out

———◆◆◆———

The most difficult part is to persevere. This is where it gets serious.

The fireworks are over. They were brilliant, but they didn't last. The light burst out and lit everything up for you, and you understood all sorts of things.

All that's left are some embers on the ground, and you have to begin again.

Now you are the rocket, and you have enough fuel to go into orbit around the earth. Easily enough to escape the force of gravity which ceaselessly draws you down to the ground again.

You thirst to live like a bird, free to love, free to give yourself and free to last out.

Last out not by clenching your teeth and trying to hold on despite the cost, but by renewing in yourself the desire to love to the end, by being faithful to your promise to look at your friend as a marvel, a priceless treasure that you will keep as such, and make fruitful.

And also by consenting to be renewed by your friend yourself. Being a treasure, he will enrich you.

Both of you will remain fragile, and all the more so if you keep your hearts open, but you will become all the stronger by refusing to close them.

———◆———